Gradu...
is Just the ...

To: _____

From: _____

Date: _____

Great Quotations, Inc.

Cover Illustration by Design Dynamics
Typography by MarketForce, Burr Ridge, IL

Published by Great Quotations Publishing Company
Glendale Heights, IL

Library of Congress Catalog number: 98-71846

ISBN 1-56245-347-5

Printed in Hong Kong 2000

I would like to dedicate this book to the Rev. Sean Charles Martin, Sr. Laura, Mr. & Mrs. Meath and all the people who have taught me so much through the years, both in and out of the classroom.

Education
is not received.
It is achieved.

"I believe that you can get everything in life you want if you will just help enough other people get what they want."

Zig Ziglar

"Destiny is not a matter of chance, it is a matter of choice; It is not a thing to be waited for, it is a thing to be achieved."

William Jennings Bryant

"It is understanding that gives us an ability to have peace. When we understand the other fellow's viewpoint, and he understands ours, then we can sit down and work out our differences."

Harry S. Truman

"How far you go in life depends on your being tender with the young, compassionate with the aged, sympathetic with the striving and tolerant of the weak and strong. Because someday you will have been all of these."

George Washington Carver

Obstacles are what
you see when you take
your eyes off your goals.

"Your living is determined not so much by what life brings to you as by the attitude you bring to life; not so much by what happens to you as by the way your mind looks at what happens." John Homer Miller

"No one can make you feel inferior without your consent." Eleanor Roosevelt

"It isn't what people think that is important, but the reason they think what they think." Eugene Ionesco

If better is possible,
good is not enough.

"What can be added to the happiness of a man who is in health, out of debt and has a clear conscience?"

Adam Smith

"It is not the employer who pays wages-he only handles the money. It is the product that pays the wages."

Henry Ford

"To be able to be caught up in the world of thought-that is being educated." Hamilton

"The gap in our economy is between what we have and what we think we ought to have-and that is a moral problem, not an economic one."

Paul Heyne

Hope sees the invisible, feels the intangible and achieves the impossible.

"Life isn't a matter of milestones but of moments."

Rose Fitzgerald Kennedy

"You have not done enough, you have never done enough, so long as it is still possible that you have something to contribute."

Dag Hammarskjold

"The secret of happiness is not found in seeking more, but in developing the capacity to enjoy less."

Dan Millman

"Nothing great will ever be achieved without great men, and men are great only if they are determined to be so."

Charles de Gaulle

"The time to repair the roof is when the sun is shining."

John F. Kennedy

"Nothing is good or bad, but thinking makes it so."

William Shakespeare

Maturity is not a
matter of age; it comes
with understanding.

The person
who marries for money
usually earns every
penny of it.

"Learn all there is to learn, and then
choose your own path."

George Friedrich Handel

"I have not failed. I have discovered
twelve hundred materials that don't work."

Thomas Edison

Quality is not an
act but a habit.
The things you do the
most are the things you
will do the best.

"It is a funny thing about life. If you refuse to accept anything but the best, you very often get it." Somerset Maugham

"Men love to wonder, and that is the seed of science." Ralph Waldo Emerson

"When has a person not felt that he knew everything, only to realize in a few years that he knew nothing?" Roderick Murchison

"People seldom improve when they have no other model but themselves to copy after."

Goldsmith

The difference
between ordinary
and extraordinary is
that little extra.

"Don't bother about genius. Don't worry about being clever. Place your trust in hard work, enthusiasm, perseverance and determination."

Sir Frederick Treves

"You can never plan the future by the past."

Edmund Burk

"It is better to light a candle than to curse the darkness."

Chinese Proverb

"All things are possible until they are proved impossible-and even the impossible may only be so as of now."

Pearl S. Buck

"If you're talkin', you ain't listenin'."

Will Rogers

"You can't build a reputation on what you're going to do."

Henry Ford

"When you come to the end of your rope, tie a knot and hang on."

Franklin D. Roosevelt

"I've never seen a monument erected to a pessimist."

Paul Harvey

Every job is a self-protrait
of the person who did it.
Autograph your
work with excellence.

"I note the obvious differences between each sort and type, but we are more alike, my friends, than we are unalike." Maya Angelou

"You learn that, whatever you are doing in life, obstacles don't matter much. Pain or other circumstances can be there, but if you want to do a job bad enough, you'll find a way to get it done."

Jack Youngblood

"He who is afraid of doing too much always does too little." German Proverb

"It is so much easier to do good than to be good." B. C. Forbes

"I know of no great man except those who have rendered great services to the human race."

Voltaire

"I play to win, whether during practice or a real game. And I will not let anything get in the way of me and my competitive enthusiasm to win."

Michael Jordan

"The truth is more important than the facts."
Frank Lloyd Wright

"I am a teacher. I do not walk on water; I do not part the sea. I just love children!"
Marva Collins

Tell me, and I'll forget.
Show me, and I may
remember. Involve me,
and I'll understand.

"Life is either a daring adventure
or nothing."

Helen Keller

"Dignity does not consist in possessing
honors, but in deserving them."

Aristotle

Before you borrow
money from
a friend, decide which
you need more.

The degree of risk is in direct proportion to the degree of return.

"There is nothing greater in life than loving another and being loved in return, for loving is the ultimate of experences."
Leo Buscaglia

"To become a father is not hard. To be a father is, however."
Wilhelm Busch

"Our greatest glory is not in never falling but in rising every time we fall."

Confucious

"We all have possibilities we don't know about. We can do things we don't even dream we can do."

Dale Carnegie

"He who does evil, expects evil."
Guinea Proverb

"A free society is one in which it is safe to be unpopular."
Adlai Stevenson

Wise people
think twice about
speaking once.

40

"Two are better than one because... if one falls down, his friend can help him up."

Ecc 4:9-10

"Truth is generally the best vindication against slander."

Abraham Lincoln

"Great minds have purpose; others have wishes."
Washington Irving

"The great thing in this world is not so much where we are but in what direction we are moving."
Oliver Wendell Holmes

"Don't throw away the old bucket until you're sure the new one holds water."
Swedish Proverb

"The man who views the world at 50 the same as he did at 20 has wasted thirty years of his life."
Muhammad Ali

"Merit begets confidence; confidence begets enthusiasm; enthusiasm conquers the world."
Walter Cottingham

"Failures are like skinned knees-painful but superficial."
H. Ross Perot

44

"Better know nothing than half-know many things."
Friedrich Nietzche

"Man is what he believes."
Anton Chekhov

"Whoever employs you does so for a selfish motive. You must be worth more to him than the money he pays you."

David Seabury

"Tomorrow is the most important thing in life. Comes into us at midnight very clean. It's perfect when it arrives and it puts itself in our hands. It hopes we've learned something from yesterday."

John Wayne

Today's preparation determines tomorrow's achievement.

"Great men
can't be ruled."
Ayn Rand

"Shallow men
believe in luck.
Strong men
believe in cause
and effect."
Emerson

"It is ill-mannered to silence a fool, and cruelty to let him go on."
Benjamin Franklin

"If you tell the truth, you don't have to remember anything."
Mark Twain

The only fool bigger than the person who knows it all is the person who argues with him.

"Everybody knows good counsel except him that has need of it."

German Proverb

"The secret of success lies not in doing your own work, but in recognizing the right man to do it."

Andrew Carnegie

"The important thing is not to stop questioning."
Albert Einstein

"All our dreams can come true, if we have the desire to pursue them."
Walt Disney

"There are no illegitimate children-only illegitimate parents."
Judge Leon R. Yankwich

"My success just evolved from working hard at the business at hand each day."
Johnny Carson

"Words without deeds have no meaning."
Tom Bradley

"Education is what survives when what has been learned has been forgotten."
B.F. Skinner

"Man must choose whether to be rich in things or in the freedom to use them."

Ivan Illich

"If you think you can, you can. If you think you can't, you're right."

Mary Kay Ash

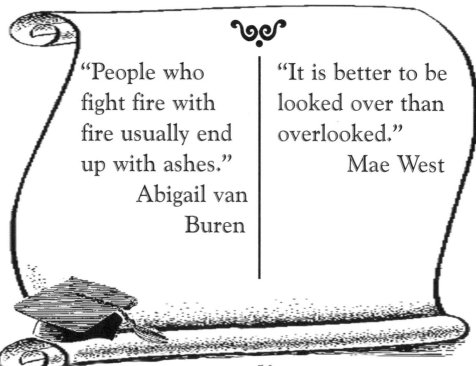

"People who fight fire with fire usually end up with ashes."
Abigail van Buren

"It is better to be looked over than overlooked."
Mae West

"We will either find a way or make one."
    Hannibal

"He who comes late must eat what is left."
    Yiddish Proverb

"Things turn out best for the people who make the best of the way things turn out."

John Wooden

"Be great in little things."

St. Francis Xavier

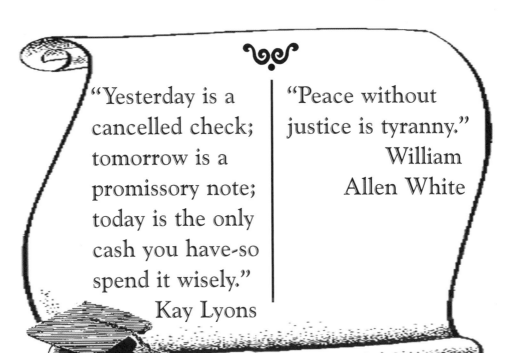

"Yesterday is a cancelled check; tomorrow is a promissory note; today is the only cash you have-so spend it wisely."
Kay Lyons

"Peace without justice is tyranny."
William Allen White

"The man who does not read good books
has no advantage over the man who can't
read them."

Mark Twain

"Hate is like acid. It can damage the
vessel in which it is stored as well as
destroy the object on which it is poured."

Ann Landers

"Courage is the price that life exacts for granting peace. The soul that knows it not, knows no release from the little things; knows not the livid loneliness of fear."

Amelia Earhart

"Show me a thoroughly satisfied man and I will show you a failure."

Thomas Alva Edison

"Creative minds have always been known to survive any kind of bad training."

Anna Freud

"Imagination is the eye of the soul."

Joseph Joubert

The person rowing
the boat seldom has
time to rock it.

"The great challenge is to prepare ourselves to enter these doors of opportunity."

Martin Luther King, Jr.

"It is only by doing things that one learns how to do things."

E. W. Scripps

"Kind words can be short and easy to speak, but their echoes are truly endless."
Mother Teresa

"Self-pity in its early stages is as snug as a feather mattress. Only when it hardens does it become uncomfortable."

Maya Angelou

"The future is so bright, it burns my eyes."

Oprah Winfrey

"If decisions were a choice between alternatives, decisions would come easy. Decision is the selection and formulation of alternatives."

Kenneth Burke

"The most important thing in communication is to hear what isn't being said."

Peter Drucker

"What hunger is in relation to food, zest is in relation to life."

Bertrand Russell

"You can't sweep people off their feet if you can't be swept off your own."

Clarence Day

"Every child is an artist. The problem is how to remain an artist once he grows up."

Pablo Picasso

"In order to have a conversation with someone, you must reveal yourself."

James Baldwin

"Standing in the middle of the road is very dangerous. You get knocked down by the traffic from both sides." Margaret Thatcher

Personality has the power to open many doors, but character keeps them open.

The journey of a
thousand miles begins
with a single step.

"When an individual is kept in a situation of inferiority, the fact is that he does become inferior."   Simone de Beauvoir

"It is easier to fight for one's principles than to live up to them."   Alfred Adler

"A problem well stated is a problem half solved."

Charles F. Kettering

"To get profit without risk, experience without danger and reward without work, is as impossible as it is to live without being born."

A. P. Gouthey

"Two things fill the mind with ever new and increasing wonder and awe-the starry heavens above me and the moral law within me."

Immanuel Kant

"Lord, grant that I may always desire more than I can accomplish."

Michelangelo

"The impersonal hand of government can never replace the helping hand of a neighbor."

Hubert H. Humphrey

"The excellent becomes the permanent."

Jane Addams

"There is a brilliant child locked inside every student."

Marva Collins

"Everyone's got it in him, if he'll only make up his mind and stick at it. None of us is born with a stop-valve on his powers or with a set limit to his capacities. There's no limit possible to the expansion of each one of us."

Charles M. Schwab

"There is no genius free from some tincture of madness."

Seneca

"What a wonderful life I've had! I only wish I'd realized it sooner."

Colette

A stranger is
only someone you
don't know yet.

"Prudence makes life safe, but it does not often make it happy."

Samuel Johnson

"Even if you're on the right track, you'll get run over if you just sit there."

Will Rogers

"A happy life is one spent in learning, earning and yearning."

Lillian Gish

"In every case, expect the sun, the moon and the stars. Settle for the sun and the moon."

Thom Munsen

"It's so hard when I have to, and so easy when I want to."

Sondra Anice Barnes

"There is no medicine like hope, no incentive so great and no tonic so powerful as expectation of something tomorrow."

Orison Swett Marden

"Very little is needed to make a happy life. It is all within yourself, in your own way of thinking."

Marcus Aurelius

"The first and best victory is to conquer self."

Plato

"Though our character is formed by circumstances, our own desires can do much to shape those circumstances; and what is really inspiriting and ennobling in the doctrine of free will is the conviction that we have real power over the formation of our own character." John Stuart Mill

"Little by little does the trick."

Aesop

"I'm a great believer in luck, and I find the harder I work the more I have of it."
Thomas Jefferson

"Don't judge any man until you have walked a mile in his moccasins."
Native American Proverb

All arguments
have two sides, but
some have no end.

"You don't start climbing a mountain to get to the middle. Why be content with being average?"

James Hart

"In reality, killing time/Is only the name for another of the multifarious ways/By which Time kills us."

Sir Osbert Sitwell

The darkest hour
is only 60 minutes.

"Though we travel the world over to find the beautiful, we must carry it with us or we find it not."
Ralph Waldo Emerson

"One never notices what has been done; one can only see what remains to be done."

Marie Curie

"Lack of fairness to an opponent is essentially a sign of weakness."
Emma Goldman

"There are just two ways of spreading light: to be the candle or the mirror that reflects it."
Edith Wharton

"In all human affairs there are efforts and there are results, and the strength of the effort is the measure of the result."
William Edward Hickson

"Where there is no vision, the people perish."
Prov 29:18

"Power can be taken, but not given. The process of the taking is empowerment in itself."
Gloria Steinem

"If history teaches anything it is that there can be not peace without equilibrium and no justice without restraint."
Henry Kissinger

"That is happiness;
to be dissolved into
something complete
and great."
Willa Cather

"Treat your friends
as you do your pic-
ture, and place
them in their best
light."

Jennie Jerome
Churchill

Blessed are those
who can give without
remembering and take
without forgetting.

"One of the weaknesses of our age is our apparent inability to distinguish our needs from our greeds."
Don Robinson

"We have to face the fact that either all of us are going to die together or we are going to learn to live together, and if we are to live together we have to talk."
Eleanor Roosevelt

"Remember wherever you go, there you are."
        Peter Weller
        The Adventures of Buckaroo Bonzai

"Your friend is the man who knows all about you and still likes you."
        Elbert Hubbard

Grant me the strength
to change the things I can,
the courage to accept the things
I can't and the wisdom to
know the difference. Serenity
Prayer

"Hold yourself responsible for a higher standard than anybody else expects of you. Never excuse yourself."
Henry
Ward Beecher

"Few men have the virtue to withstand the highest bidder."
George Washington

"He that lies down with dogs will rise up with fleas."
Barber

"One can never consent to creep when one feels an impulse to soar."
Helen Keller

Doers get to the top
of the oak tree by
climbing it. Dreamers
sit on an acorn.

"If the airplane I'm in is about to crash into the side of a mountain, I'm not going to sit around and complain with my fellow passengers. I'm going to sit in the pilot's chair and pull up on the stick."
Ron Dreiling

"If you bungle raising your children, I don't think whatever else you do well matters very much."

Jacqueline Kennedy-Onassis

"Nothing is as real as a dream. The world can change around you, but your dreams will not. Responsibilities need not erase it. Duties need not obscure it. Because the dream is within you, no one can take it away."
Tom Clancy

"From now on, any definition of a successful life must include serving others."
George Bush

"Strong lives are motivated by dynamic purposes." Kenneth Hildebrand.

"No person was ever honored for what he received; honor has been the reward for what he gave." Calvin Coolidge

"Each man should frame life so that at some future hour fact and his dreamings meet."
Victor Hugo

"Love doesn't make the world go 'round. Love is what makes the ride worthwhile."
Franklin P. Jones

"Poetry is not the assertion of truth, but the making of that truth fully real to us."
T. S. Eliot

"Who can say what new horizons lie before us if we can but maintain the initiative and develop the imagination to penetrate them?"
Alfred P. Sloan

"Must the hunger become anger and the anger fury before anything will be done?"
John Steinbeck

"Life is about not knowing, having to change, taking the moment and making the best of it, without knowing what's going to happen next. Delicious ambiguity."
Gilda Radner

"It took me a long time not to judge myself through someone else's eyes."
Sally Field

"Life is no brief candle to me. It is a sort of splendid torch which I have got hold of for a moment, and I want to make it burn as brightly as possible before handing it on to future generations."
George Bernard Shaw

"We judge ourselves by what we feel capable of doing, while others judge us be what we have already done."
Henry Wadsworth Longfellow

"Everything has been figured out except how to live."
Jean-Paul Sartre

"Great men are meteors designed to burn so that earth may be lighted."
Napoleon Bonaparte

"Only the shallow know themselves."
Oscar Wilde

"Looking back, my life seems like one long obstacle race, with me as its chief obstacle."
Jack Paar

"A lot of the problems of America are problems of the spirit. I believe they can only be solved when people are dealing with each other one on one, and when we reconnect and we reach across the lines that divide us."
Bill Clinton

"A man with wisdom is better off than a stupid man with any amount of charm."
African Proverb

"The price of freedom is eternal vigilance."
Frederick Douglas

"The best things and the best people rise out of their separateness; I'm against a homogenized society because I want the cream to rise."
Robert Frost

"You don't save a pitcher for tomorrow. Tomorrow it may rain."
Leo Durocher

"Statistics are for losers."
Scotty Bowman

"To teach is to learn."
Japanese Proverb

"If I had to give young writers advice, I'd say don't listen to writers talking about writing."
Lillian Hellman

"I do not feel obligated to believe that that same God who has endowed us with sense, reason and intellect has intended us to forego their use."
Galileo Galilei

"It takes 20 years to make an overnight success."

Eddie Cantor

"A strong passion for any object will ensure success, for the desire of the end well point out the means."

William Hazlitt

"Failure is painful but short-lived, but regret is a question you will answer the rest of your life." Ashley Netreba

"You have to know you can win. You have to think you can win. You have to feel you can win."

Sugar Ray Leonard

"We can achieve nothing without paying the price."

Earl Nightingale

At any one moment, we have more possibilities than we have ability to act upon.

"I can give you a six-word formulaor success: Think things through then follow through."

Eddie Rickenbacker

"We don't see things are they as, we see things as we are."

Anais Nin

"When you get into a tight place and every-thing goes against you, till it seems as though you could not hang on a minute longer, never give up then, for that is just the place and time that the tide will turn."

Harriet Beecher Stowe

"If you don't know where you're going, any path will take you there."

Sioux Proverb

"Never try to take the manners of another as your own, for the theft will be immediately evident and the thief will appear as ridiculous as a robin with peacock feathers hastily stuck on."

Maya Angelou

"Surely a man has come to himself only when he has found the best that is in him, and has satisfied his heart with the highest achievement he is fit for."

Woodrow Wilson

"No one can possibly achieve any real and lasting success or get rich in business by being a conformist content with reality."

J. Paul Getty

"Take calculated risks. That is quite different from being rash."

George S. Patton

"Through zeal, knowledge is gotten;
through lack of zeal, knowledge is lost."

Buddha

"Advice is seldom welcome, and those who
need it the most, like it the least."

Lord Chesterfield

Character is
determined by what
you accomplish when
the excitement is gone.

"Treasure the love you receive above all.
It will survive long after your gold and
good health have vanished." Og Mandino

"Peace cannot be kept by force. It can
only be achieved by understanding."

Albert Einstein

"The person who talks most of his own virtue is often the least virtuous."

Jawaharial Nehru

"They conquer who believe they can."

John Dryden

"Dignity consists not in possessing honors, but in the consciousness that we deserve them."

Aristotle

"Until justice is blind to color, until education is unaware of race, until opportunity is unconcerned with the color of men's skin, emancipation will be a proclamation but not a fact."

Lyndon B. Johnson

The greatest danger for most of us is not that our aim is too high and we miss it, but that our aim is too low and we reach it.

"If the misery of others leaves you indifferent and with no feeling of sorrow, then you cannot be called a human being."

Jimmy Carter

"Taking a new step, uttering a new word, is what people fear most."

Fyodor Dostoevsky

"The bigger a man's head, the worse his headache."

Persian Proverb

"We can't all be heroes because somebody has to sit on the curb and clap as they go by."

Will Rogers

"Stability is not mobility."

Klemmons von Metternich

"Rockne wanted nothing but 'bad losers.'
Good losers get into the habit of losing."

George E. Allen

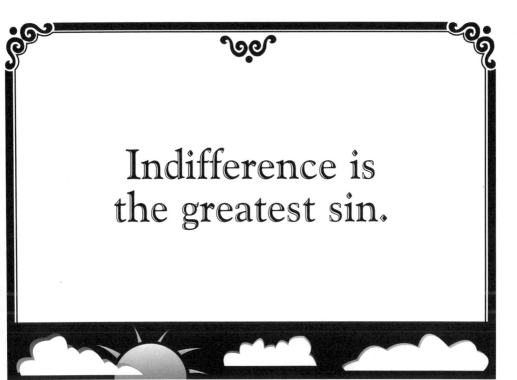

Indifference is
the greatest sin.

In order to
have friends, you
must first be one.

"You may go where you wish, but you cannot escape yourself." Norwegian Proverb

"Associate with individuals of good quality if you esteem your own reputation, for it is better to be alone than in bad company."
George Washington

"There is only one success-to spend your life your way."

Christopher Morley

"A successful marriage is an edifice that must be rebuilt every day."

Andre Maurols

Some succeed because they are destined to, but most succeed because they are determined to.

"Courtesies of a small and trivial character are the ones which strike deepest in the grateful and appreciating heart."

Henry Clay

"You will find as you look back upon your life that the moments when you have really lived are the moments when you have done things in the spirit of love."

Henry Drummond

"I will not permit any man to narrow and degrade my soul by making me hate him."

Booker T. Washington

"The miracle is this: the more we share, the more we have."

Leonard Nimoy

"Mix a conviction with a man and something happens." Adam Clayton Powell

"I have made mistakes but I have never made the mistake of claiming that I never made one." James Gordon Bennett

"The trouble with life in the fast lane is that you get to the other end in an awful hurry."   John Jensen

"The future has several names. For the weak, it is the impossible. For the faint-hearted, it is the unknown. For the thoughtful and valiant, it is the ideal."
                                              Victor Hugo

"If you want happiness for an hour, take a nap. If you want happiness for a day, go fishing. If you want happiness for a month, get married. If you want happiness for a year, inherit a fortune. If you want happiness for a lifetime, help someone else."

Chinese Proverb

"Everyone has inside of him a piece of good news. The good news is that you don't know how great you can be! How much you can love! What you can accomplish! And what your potential is!"

Anne Frank

"The barriers are not erected which can say to an aspiring talents and industry: Thus far and no farther."

Ludwig van Beethoven

"We know what we are, but we know not what we may be."

William Shakespeare

"If we all did the things we are capable of doing, we would literally astound ourselves."

Thomas Edison

To the optimist,
a fireplace is a center
of warmth and beauty.
To the pessimist, it
is a source of smoke
and ashes.

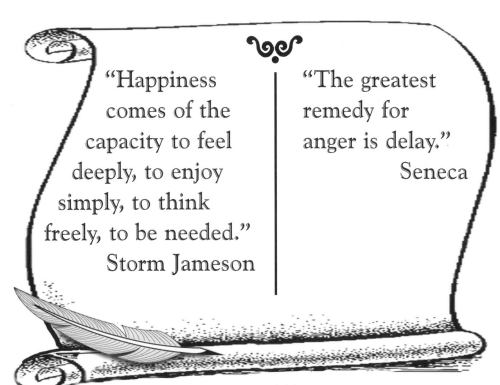

"Happiness comes of the capacity to feel deeply, to enjoy simply, to think freely, to be needed."
Storm Jameson

"The greatest remedy for anger is delay."
Seneca

144

"I think it's the end of progress if you stand still and think of what you've done in the past. I keep on."

Leslie Caron

"Reformers who are always compromising, have not yet grasped the idea that truth is the only safe ground to stand upon."

Elizabeth Cady Stanton

"The surest way to make a name for yourself is to find out where the crowd is going and then run the other way."
Joseph P. Martin

"A man either lives life as it happens to him, meets it head-on and licks it, or he turns his back on it and starts to wither away."
Gene Roddenberry

"Human rights rest on human dignity. The dignity of an individual is an ideal worth fighting for and worth dying for"
Robert Mayard

"Winning isn't everything, but wanting to win is."
Vince Lombardi

"Chance favors the prepared mind."
Louis Pasteur

"To possess ideas is to gather flowers. To think is to weave them into garlands."
Greek Proverb

One does
not find happiness
in marriage, but
takes happiness
into marriage.

"I have observed that to succeed in the world one should appear like a fool but be wise."

Montesquieu

"The only limit to our realization of tomorrow will be our doubts of today."

Franklin Delano Roosevelt

"Life's an open book, and an education helps you write success stories."
Joyce A. Myers

"Mistakes are part of the dues one pays for a full life."
Sophia Loren

"A man is a success if he gets up in the morning and goes to bed at night and in between does what he wants to do."
Bob Dylan

"Joy comes from using your potential."
Will Schultz

"Nothing is really work unless you would rather be doing something else."
James M. Barrie

"Those who condemn wealth are those who have none and see no chance of getting it."
William Penn Patrick

"Be slow in choosing a friend, slower in changing."
Benjamin Franklin

"When you look for the good in others, you discover the best in yourself."
Martin Walsh

"To be persuasive, we must be believable. To be believable, we must be credible. To be credible, we must be truthful."
Edward R. Murrow

"As long as you're green, you're growing; as soon as you're ripe, you start to rot."
Ray Kroc

"The human spirit needs to accomplish, to achieve, to triumph to be happy."

Ben Stein

"What a man really wants is creative challenge with sufficient skills to bring him within the reach of success so that he may have the expanding joy of achievement."

Fay B. Nash

To know what
is right and not
do it is as bad as
doing wrong.

Be a leader!
Remember - the lead
sled dog is the only
one with a decent view.

"Happiness is inward, and not outward; and so, it does not depend on what we have, but what we are."

Henry Van Dyke

"Small deeds done are better than great deeds planned."

Peter Marshall

"Take away love and our earth is a tomb."

Robert Browning

"Fear is met and destroyed with courage."

James F. Bell

"There is no such thing as a self-made man. You will reach your goals only with the help of others."

George Shinn

"If you don't run your own life, somebody else will."

John Atkinson

"Confidence doesn't come out of nowhere. It's a result of something...hours and days and weeks and years of constant work and dedication."
Roger Staubach

"Sometimes if you want to see a change for the better, you have to take things into your own hands."
Clint Eastwood

"We can chart our future clearly and wisely only when we know the path which has led to the present."

Adlai Stevenson

"A man without knowledge of himself and his heritage is like a tree without roots."

Dick Gregory

"If you escape from people too often, you wind up escaping from yourself."
Marvin Gaye

"If a man sought a companion who acted entirely like himself, he would live in solitude."
Nigerian Proverb

"Life gives nothing to man without labor."
Horace

"If you keep saying that things are going to be bad, you have a chance of being a prophet."
Isaac Singer

Hope sees the invisible, feels the intangible and achieves the impossible.

"Be truthful, one would say, and the result is bound to be amazingly interesting. Comedy is bound to be enriched. New facts are bound to be discovered."

Virginia Woolf

"Neither the wise man nor a brave man lies down on the tracks of history to wait for the train of the future to run over him."

Dwight D. Eisenhower

Other Titles by Great Quotations

301 Ways to Stay Young At Heart
African-American Wisdom
A Lifetime of Love
A Light Heart Lives Long
Angel-grams
As A Cat Thinketh
A Servant's Heart
Astrology for Cats
Astrology for Dogs
A Teacher is Better Than Two Books
A Touch of Friendship
Can We Talk
Celebrating Women
Chicken Soup
Chocoholic Reasonettes
Daddy & Me
Dare to Excel
Erasing My Sanity
Falling in Love
Fantastic Father, Dependable Dad
Golden Years, Golden Words
Graduation Is Just The Beginning
Grandma, I Love You
Happiness is Found Along The Way

High Anxieties
Hooked on Golf
I Didn't Do It
Ignorance is Bliss
I'm Not Over the Hill
Inspirations
Interior Design for Idiots
Let's Talk Decorating
Life's Lessons
Life's Simple Pleasures
Looking for Mr. Right
Midwest Wisdom
Mommy & Me
Mom's Homemade Jams
Mother, I Love You
Motivating Quotes for Motivated People
Mrs. Murphy's Laws
Mrs. Webster's Dictionary
My Daughter, My Special Friend
Only a Sister
Parenting 101
Pink Power
Read the Fine Print

Reflections
Romantic Rhapsody
Size Counts !
Social Disgraces
Sports Prose
Stress or Sanity
The ABC's of Parenting
The Be-Attitudes
The Birthday Astrologer
The Cornerstones of Success
The Rose Mystique
The Secret Language of Men
The Secret Language of Women
The Secrets in Your Face
The Secrets in Your Name
TeenAge of Insanity
Thanks from the Heart
The Lemonade Handbook
The Mother Load
The Other Species
Wedding Wonders
Words From The Coach
Working Woman's World

Great Quotations Publishing Company

1967 Quincy Court
Glendale Heights, IL 60139, U.S.A.
Phone: 630-582-2800   Fax: 630-582-2813
http://www.greatquotations.com